HOW TO
RETIRE
RICH
AND
LOOK
POOR
IN RETIREMENT

HOW TO RETIRE RICH AND LOOK POOR

IN RETIREMENT

Chris Heerlein

HOW TO RETIRE RICH AND LOOK POOR IN RETIREMENT

The Millionaire's Tax Playbook

© 2026 by Chris Heerlein

REAP Financial Group, LLC is an SEC-registered investment advisory firm helping individuals create retirement strategies using a variety of investment and insurance products to meet their needs and objectives.

ISBN-13: 978-1-966168-65-2
Library of Congress Control Number: 2026902164

Designed by Melissa Farr, Back Porch Creative, LLC

WEALTH AUTHORITY BOOKS
2511 WOODLANDS WAY
OCEANSIDE, CA 92054
www.indiebooksintl.com

Wealth Authority Books is an imprint of Indie Books International®, Inc.

Table Of Contents

The Top Seven Things Most Retirees Get Wrong When Planning For Retirement

Everyone wants to avoid mistakes when planning their retirement. Below are the top seven things most retirees get wrong.

1. Underestimating The Importance Of Longevity

When planning for retirement, many people assume they won't live as long as they actually might. It's easy to look at your retirement plans and assume you won't make it into your nineties and beyond. However, it's crucial to plan so you have enough wealth and cash flow to outlast you. This enables you to leave money for your loved ones or avoid becoming a financial burden. When you make your retirement plan, don't underestimate the importance of longevity.

This also applies to Social Security timing. The money you stand to receive from Social Security is massive, so you want to factor longevity into your Social Security claiming strategy.

2. Ignoring Inflation

In recent years, we've experienced high inflation in the United States. Prices for services and goods have gone up significantly. Due to these increasing prices, inflation has been more apparent in recent history than in the past. Despite this, many people preparing for retirement forget to factor inflation into their plans. Your budget should account for inflation over time. REAP Financial recommends that you base your projections on long-term historical averages and assume a minimum 3 percent inflation rate per year.

We always stress that inflation does not make you broke, but it may reduce your lifestyle and standard of living. If you want to maintain or increase your standard of living in retirement, accounting for inflation is essential.

3. Being Overly Optimistic Or Pessimistic About The Market

Since your retirement plans will revolve around expected returns for your portfolio, we encourage our clients to maintain a neutral outlook on the market. For example, assuming a 10 percent annual return on your retirement portfolio may leave you unprepared if the market underperforms. It might be better to assume a more modest 5–6 percent rate of return, so your estimates are conservative.

On the opposite side, we don't want you to be overly pessimistic either. Many people make investment decisions out of fear, driven by emotions. You should aim to avoid letting emotions dictate your financial decisions. This is one of the crucial services we provide at REAP Financial, helping clients remove emotions from their financial decisions.

4. Not Understanding Social Security And The Importance Of Timing

Social Security was mentioned briefly above, but it's so important that it's worth mentioning twice. You need to have a strategy concerning when you'll take your Social Security, based on your expected longevity. Today, more and more people are in a position where they might benefit from not waiting to take their benefit. While this strategy isn't suitable for everyone, a general rule of thumb is that individuals with a net worth exceeding $2–$3 million may find it advantageous to claim Social Security early. This is an analysis we do for our clients at REAP Financial to give them confidence in their Social Security claiming strategy, since it's such an important part of overall retirement planning.

5. Not Preparing For Healthcare Costs

In retirement, healthcare costs are expensive, and they need to be built into your budget. When we're considering Medicare in particular, Medicare premiums are determined by your income. That means you may be paying hundreds more for your Medicare coverage, depending on your income. You'll also want to consider potential long-term care, nursing home care, and home healthcare costs. Although these situations are difficult to think about, later-life care expenses can rapidly diminish your portfolio due to increased drawdown rates and associated tax implications. For these reasons, it's important to understand the short-, medium-, and long-term healthcare costs you'll face in retirement.

6. Overspending Without A Budget

The most important number in your retirement plan is your budget. If you don't have a budget, you risk depleting your portfolio too early. We strive to ensure your budget aligns with what your portfolio can sustain through the years. Budgeting isn't as critical when you're working, since you're always bringing money in. However, when you retire and your cash flow is constricted, the budget becomes crucially important. Don't underestimate the importance of your budget.

7. Trying To Have A DIY Retirement Plan

We tend to meet families in their fifties and sixties when they're considering a transition to retirement. Some families are even forced into retirement by health conditions or other life circumstances. All of this is to say, retirement is a different ball game, and there are lots of factors that go into it, as we've mentioned above. Tax and retirement planning can become more complex when most of your wealth is in IRAs or 401(k)s. One way to manage your tax bracket in retirement is through Roth conversions, but these conversions can impact your taxable income in retirement. For these reasons, it is essential you work with a qualified fiduciary advisor who can guide you through the process.

Working The Millionaire's Playbook

These seven areas to consider are just scratching the surface of retiring rich while looking poor. What follows is the culmination of decades of work and research. This is an expression of my passion to make the enjoyment of your retirement everything you imagined it would be and more.

Note: Some of the data related to tax code, such as contribution minimums, maximums, and age cutoffs, will change over time and as new laws take effect. Such numbers and data used here are for demonstration purposes only.

PART ONE

PROTECTING WEALTH

FROM THE

STEALTH TAX

You've Earned It–
Here's How To Keep It

High-net-worth individuals face particular challenges in strategizing to manage wealth. If you've saved $2 million to $20 million, you've done the hard work.

All of that heavy lifting did not happen by accident. You saved until it hurt, and then you saved some more. You took advantage of every 401(k) offered by the companies you worked for. You and your spouse opened some IRAs and a brokerage account. You managed to sock away multiple millions. Now, retirement is on the horizon, and you want to make the most of it. With a tidy nest egg, what could you possibly have to worry about?

When you have $2 million to $20 million, you are not likely to have a money problem, but you will likely have a significant tax problem. It blindsides even the most successful savers. They spoke with a financial planner now and then, but never had a significant conversation about taxes beyond deferral through retirement savings instruments. Some advisors function as what I call "accumulators." Their only job is to grow accounts as fast as possible, but what happens when the paychecks stop?

The problem is that, as I write this, the United States is experiencing the lowest tax rates in over forty years. People in this situation sell a business or otherwise retire without thinking about the tax implications. However, even as income stops, they remain in either the same tax bracket or a higher one. That's happening right now when tax rates are at their lowest. When people started saving in the '80s and '90s, taxes were much higher than they are now. An increase in taxes would have been understandable, but instead, they have decreased.

So, will people be in the same tax bracket or a higher one when they retire? That's what the majority of high-net-worth households need to know when planning for retirement, not just about accumulating wealth. If you're only making double-digit returns year over year in order to just pay them out as taxes, what's the point? What are we doing if you've got no advanced planning to keep the wealth in the family?

How do you avoid overpaying Uncle Sam so you can leave more money to the causes you believe in or those you love and make a real impact in this world?

We all hate paying taxes, but there needs to be a strategy beyond deferment. Putting savings into an IRA or 401(k) is all about deferment. Believe it or not, *where* you save is more important than *how much* you save. Again, even if taxation stays historically low, you could potentially be in the same or a higher tax bracket in retirement. How likely is it that taxes will stay low in the future? Not very.

The sooner you realize you have a tax problem, even if you don't have a money problem, the sooner you can work toward a solution. Here is the challenge, starkly put: Your net worth may appear to be, say, $6 million on paper, but it's not. It's worth $4.5 million after Uncle Sam takes his cut. You need to think about the *net* total of your assets, not the gross total.

This is not the worst problem in the world to have, but if you want to keep more of what is already yours, I will show you the methods and strategies to help make that happen. There are no quick fixes, but by starting as soon as possible, you can mitigate your tax exposure in retirement.

> Your retirement statement shows your gross wealth. What truly matters is the net amount you get to keep after taxes.

If we do it right, you'll be able to enjoy the fruits of your labor in retirement and leave more to heirs and causes that inspire you.

I get it. You are used to thinking in terms of rates of return. That's the easy part. However, if you've got no plan to keep it in the family, what have we been doing for years? This is the commonality with our clients: We have no problem paying our fair share in taxes, but no more than our fair share. That's the mindset.

Three Types Of Money

We've been paying our fair share for decades. In retirement, wouldn't it be great to pay attention so you don't overpay in taxes? Not overpaying starts with a basic understanding of money and taxes.

There are three types of money: There is money that is always taxed, like one's income, pension, and IRA distributions. There is money that is sometimes taxed, like cash savings at the bank, capital gains on investments, and Social Security income. Then, there is money that is never taxed, like a Roth IRA and Roth 401(k).

For the average investor, the latter is the smallest part of the portfolio; US consumers have been programmed for the immediate. We want to save taxes today.

The question more people need to ask themselves is: how do we rearrange things now to save millions of dollars over thirty or so years of retirement?

Let's look at Medicare as an example. If you have accumulated at least several million dollars, you are potentially going to pay more for your Medicare premiums than your neighbor. You may pay $680 a month while your neighbor is paying $380. If you and your spouse pay that amount over thirty years, that's hundreds of thousands of dollars more than the average American pays.

How can this be fixed? It can be done by keeping what is listed as income to a minimum. You can legally look "poor" on paper. The current laws in this country are written around your income and not your net worth. That's why you want to get poor on paper legally and easily.

In the following chapter, I'm going to go into detail about how Medicare functions as a "stealth tax" in retirement.[1] The issue with stealth taxes is that you don't see them coming, and they are almost invisible on your tax return. These things don't increase your tax bracket. Without careful planning, you are on the hook for more taxes or stealth taxes while remaining in the same tax bracket.

I want high-net-worth people to know how to retire rich and look poor. These are not "trade secrets" that you will need a tax attorney to implement on your behalf. They are tested strategies I have been helping people discover for well over a decade. Now it's your turn to learn and put these strategies into practice.

2

The American Stealth Tax

The American stealth tax is something that most retirees face. Many don't see it coming until it's too late. The laws in this country are written around income, not so much your net worth. If you have a nice lifestyle you're looking to maintain and you've got a lot of income coming in through pensions, royalties, dividends, et cetera, your income may end up being higher than you think in retirement.

Are we talking about actual taxes here? The short answer is not literally. We are talking about stealth taxes—indirect taxation that may go unnoticed by you, the person who pays it.[2] Many people may not call it a tax, but because it results in more of your money going to the government through Social Security taxes and higher Medicare premiums, it feels just like a tax.

> A "stealth tax" isn't on your 1040 form—
> it's the extra money you unknowingly send
> back to the government through things
> like higher Medicare premiums.

Let's take a closer look at how Medicare serves as a stealth tax. Your income dictates your Medicare premiums, which are based on your tax return from the two years before. As of this writing, if your modified income from two years ago was over $109,000 (for single filers) or if you're married and you report over $218,000 in income, monthly Medicare premiums will increase. There are six income tiers that determine these premium increases, known as the Income-Related Monthly Adjustment amount (IRMAA). It's not just your Part B premiums; it's also your Medicare Part D premiums and your drug plan.

To avoid this stealth tax, you must keep your Medicare premiums at the bare minimum throughout retirement. That means keeping all the categories of income in retirement at a minimum.

Social Security payments are income. Believe it or not, even the tax-free interest on municipal bonds counts as income. A pension is definitely income. Add to this your short- and long-term capital gains.

You may think you are a long way from $218,000 in income, but when you add it all up, you are in for a surprise. Once again, the tax laws in this country are based on your income, not your net worth. I want you to have millions in the bank but be poor on the bottom line of your 1040.

It is also a good idea to keep an eye on future earnings. As inflation goes up, you will need to pull more money out of your retirement accounts. Whether you have an IRA or 401(k), it's all taxable as income. For example, you may need to sell assets in retirement, such as company stock from a highly appreciated brokerage account or even your primary home. These capital gains count toward these Medicare thresholds.

These events happen every year. Whether it is selling a house or some other asset, if you have a capital event, that gain counts toward income thresholds. Before you know it, you could be paying several hundred more a month per person for Medicare.

If you were to go to the very top tier, you could be paying well over $670 a month per person. So, for a married couple, that could easily be close to $10,000 more in Medicare premiums in a given year.

A single large transaction, like selling a home or company stock, can unexpectedly spike your Medicare premiums for years to come.

To be clear, if you find yourself in this situation, you are not stuck paying higher premiums forever. This is all based on income, so if you find yourself paying higher Medicare premiums, you need to find ways to bring down your income. Medicare looks back at your income from your tax return filed two years prior, meaning your current premium is based on your income from two years ago; this is referred to as the "Medicare look-back period," where the Social Security Administration uses your modified adjusted gross income (MAGI) from that tax return to calculate your premium amount.

If the bulk of your wealth is in IRAs and 401(k)s, that money continues to grow throughout the years. Under today's law, required minimum distributions (RMDs) begin at age seventy-three for those who turn seventy-two after December 31, 2022, and will increase to age seventy-five starting in 2033. You are required to take a certain amount from your IRAs and 401(k)s, whether you need that money to support your lifestyle or not. You guessed it, these dollars count as income.

With large tax-deferred accounts, your RMD could be $40,000 per year. It may be $65,000. It could be $125,000. We have clients with over $200,000 annually in required distributions, and that's all income.

Another thing to be aware of is that your tax bracket may shift with these RMDs. You may find yourself in a 22 percent bracket from age sixty-two to seventy-two, and when your required distribution kicks in, boom, that extra cash in hand may accelerate your tax bracket.

I love this country. I do not have a problem paying my fair share of taxes, but no more. When people retire, they often assume taxes will become incredibly simple because the W-2 paycheck goes away. I can tell you right now, particularly for those who have saved diligently, taxes can become much more complicated in retirement.

The word *stealth*, believe it or not, is derived from the word steal. It's true. When it comes to the American stealth tax, utilizing the opportunities available to get around it can add a dramatic amount of dollars and success to a family's retirement.

Now, you're starting to connect the dots on why I call this an American stealth tax. Do not let healthcare expenses derail your retirement. The good news is that by planning ahead, there are ways that you can reposition your portfolio to keep your required distributions down and have the control you seek in retirement. Use the QR code below to get a free copy of my *Medicare 101*.

3

The Paper Trail Of Wealthy Retirees
What You Need To Know

As you read this chapter, consider the lessons from the superrich and what the wealthiest can teach us. What do the wealthiest Americans, those with $25 million or more of net worth, think about life? What do they think about when it comes to values, family, money, and more? Knowing these answers can be very beneficial to you.[3]

One clear finding is that the successful families we work with are constantly educating themselves. They want to get better every day. It is easy to assume that people with great wealth may only have goals that are purely financial in nature. The ultrawealthy care a great deal about living their best lives, which includes living a life aligned with their values and having fulfilling relationships with family and friends.

In some of this polling of the ultrawealthy, 66 percent said that living a life that aligns with one's values is the most important thing, and 54 percent said having fulfilling relationships with family and friends is the most important. Now, not surprisingly, given their wealth, fewer than half cited financial issues like being financially stable and secure, and having money for the unexpected.

The wealthiest families never stop learning. They treat financial wisdom as a lifelong pursuit, not a destination.

More surprisingly, just a quarter of the wealthy individuals polled included early retirement in their definition of their best life. Consider checking in with yourself and the important people in your life about the goals that really matter to you individually and collectively. If you have far less than $25 million in net worth, you may find yourself prioritizing goals such as being financially secure, and that may be top of the list for you. Be sure to make room for the things that constitute a great life for many of us, such as living your values, spending time with family and friends, staying healthy, and doing meaningful work to stay active and sharp.

Like everybody else, the ultrawealthy have their share of worries and concerns. Some may look extremely familiar to you, even if you're far less wealthy. For example, the CEG Worldwide study found that the ultrawealthy harbor significant concerns about preserving and protecting their wealth overall: 84 percent of people polled were worried about rising interest rates, 77 percent were anxious about maintaining their current financial position, and 74 percent were concerned about their performance in the stock market.[4] It is easy to imagine that as your wealth increases, you are more likely to be concerned about those issues.

The ultrawealthy also have the well-being of their families on their minds. Among family-related issues, concern about funding their children's and grandchildren's education ranks first at 65 percent, tied with leaving a legacy for their heirs. This is followed by passing down key values to the next generation, at 63 percent. Chances are, you and many of our clients share some or maybe all of these concerns.

One of the findings that really stood out was that a large percentage of the ultra-affluent—47 percent—are worried about divorce, possibly because the size of their wealth may be much smaller on the other side.

Then there are concerns around health. The research shows that having money doesn't make you immune to health worries. This group of high-net-worth individuals is worried about their own health, the health of their spouse and family, and a range of other issues.

It was interesting to see in this research that, in most cases, concerns about health increase along with the net worth. For example, 82 percent of those with a net worth of $125 million or more are worried about their health, versus just 70 percent overall. Clearly, even though the substantial wealth of this group likely enables them to secure expertise and resources to respond to many health and long-term care challenges, they remain very concerned about those issues.

The takeaway from this data is that you should have candid conversations about health. This could include discussing how to prepare financially for potential illness, and the cost of healthcare and long-term care down the road. When we build plans at REAP Financial, one of the first things we examine is whether you have enough money in late life to self-insure to pay for long-term care. Many of our clients have long-term care policies. Some come to realize they can self-insure and no longer carry them.

When you think about healthcare and later life, it makes a lot of sense to have a conversation with your advisor and your estate attorney about powers of attorney, living will trusts, and other estate planning tools. If you are particularly concerned about a spouse's health or a family health catastrophe, consider having family discussions about health and finances with children and other loved ones.

When it comes to spending and investing, it's not surprising that the ultrawealthy have strong opinions about their money and how to manage it best. Case in point, nearly four out of five of the ultrawealthy—78 percent—attribute their happiness in large part to the wealth they've accumulated. Nearly 85 percent report that they get greater satisfaction from saving and investing wealth than from spending it. At the highest wealth level of $125 million or more, that figure is even higher at 92 percent.

That said, the ultrawealthy don't simply hoard their money. How they spend it really might surprise you. More than 20 percent of these investors don't spend a single dollar on many items commonly associated with the wealthy. They are not spending big on things like exotic cars, boats, jewelry, collectibles, gambling, or political contributions.

Looking at categories with significant annual spending, like $25,000 or more, charitable donations are the top expenditure, with around 51 percent donating at least $25,000 a year to charity. One in eight, around 15 percent, donated more than $100,000 in the past year.

Now, you'll appreciate this: vacation spending came in a close second, with about 47 percent spending at least $25,000 a year on vacation. Home improvements were another significant expenditure, with 42 percent spending at least $25,000 or more over the past twelve months on improvements. Despite their fairly high levels of concern about funding the education of children or grandchildren, 36 percent spend nothing on college tuition, and 41 percent spend nothing on private prep schools.

The truly wealthy know that fulfillment comes from investing in experiences and charitable giving, not just accumulating possessions.

Whatever your own key concerns, make sure your plan is designed to address those issues. Consider your own preferences when it comes to investing in wealth and managing it in other ways. Are you as involved in wealth management as you'd like to be, or would you prefer to take a more hands-on approach? Conversely, would you rather hand off the duties to professionals? That's where many of our clients are at with REAP Financial. They've done the work, and they're looking to transition into retirement and enjoy their wealth.

That's why we've planned with so many people over the years: to help them enjoy spending their wealth because they can spend it confidently, knowing they are getting the most from their money.

Examine where your money goes. Ask yourself, "Am I spending it in ways that are meaningful to me, ways that bring me closer to living what I define as my best life?"

I think the ultra-affluent are really onto something with their spending patterns. Research beyond our own shows that people report greater happiness when they make experiential purchases, such as vacations, than when they buy physical items like clothing and furniture.[5] Other research shows that prosocial spending, such as charitable contributions, is linked with higher levels of well-being and satisfaction.

At the end of the day, I'm a believer that we can all learn a great deal from each other. When it comes to issues such as living our best life, spending wisely, and addressing important concerns, knowing what the ultrawealthy are thinking and doing serves as a road map for our very own decision-making.

4

Why Your Retirement Tax Bracket Might Shock You

When you are working, taxes are fairly uncomplicated. You're getting a W-2 paycheck. Taxes are being withheld. You may be contributing to your 401(k) at work, qualifying for a tax deduction.

When you retire, taxes can get much more complicated. Many retirees fall into tax traps that they never saw coming, which results in unnecessary interest and penalties.

Even though taxes get more complicated in retirement, you can gain more control over your taxes in retirement than at any time in your life, if you know what you're doing. Retirees often find themselves paying more taxes than needed or more penalties and interest throughout the years than needed.

As I mentioned, when you're working, you receive a paycheck, and taxes are withheld accordingly. It's straightforward. When you retire, you've got a portfolio that might consist of CDs, a money market fund, cash, brokerage accounts, IRAs, 401(k)s, Roth IRAs, and HSAs. All these things are taxed differently, but you get to decide which ones you want to live on and in what sequence you're going to withdraw from them. That's where we can optimize things.

More Bad News: The Widow(er)'s Penalty

The widow(er)'s penalty, as the name implies, happens when someone loses a spouse. You might find yourself in this situation, or maybe you have elderly parents to whom this could happen. Why is losing a spouse a potentially taxable event? Because the tax laws in this country are favorable for those who file jointly. Once you file as a single person, the tax bracket shift is dramatic.

The "widow(er)'s penalty" is a harsh reality: losing a spouse can instantly push the survivor into a much higher tax bracket, even if their lifestyle hasn't changed.

We see the widow(er)'s penalty occur the year after losing a spouse. When this happens, wealth shrinks seemingly overnight because the new single-person brackets create more taxation. Typically, one's budget and lifestyle don't change too much after a spouse passes. You will see some income loss, particularly if you lose a pension or a Social

Security check from your spouse. Generally, your budget doesn't change that much, but your brackets do.

This means the income you are living on is being assessed at a higher rate of tax. If you jump brackets, more of your Social Security check will likely go back to the government. Remember, too, that under current thresholds, when you earn over $109,000 a year in income as a single filer, your Medicare premiums go up. Losing a spouse, in addition to the emotional toll, creates a kind of snowball effect around potential taxes.

Estimated Tax Penalties

One more reason to pay close attention to your tax bracket in retirement is estimated tax payment penalties. Estimated tax payment penalties are assessed when you don't evenly make estimated tax payments throughout the year. When you received a W-2 paycheck, taxes were withheld evenly throughout the year. However, in retirement, if you're taking money from your IRAs and 401(k)s and not withholding tax, that can create interest penalties, plus a big tax bomb at the end of the year.

You can set up quarterly payments to avoid this trap. If you're taking distributions from these pretax accounts, you can easily set up withholding on those accounts, and I recommend it.

You are also earning interest in savings accounts, money markets, and CDs. That's money you're usually not even using, just reinvesting the interest or dividends, but it is considered income. If you invest in mutual funds in your brokerage accounts, that can also be considered income; those distributions, and/or if the mutual fund managers buy and sell, can create ordinary and qualified dividends.

If you have these types of investments in your portfolio, you will be expected to pay estimated tax payments in retirement. For instance, if you sold company stock or highly appreciated stock in February, your first estimated tax payment would be due on April 15. Next is June 15, then September 15, then January 15.

Here's another example: If you did a large Roth conversion at the end of the year, let's say in October or November, you would be required to make an estimated tax payment on that by January 15 of the upcoming year. Many retirees do not think about these kinds of events as income.

There is a potential remedy for these kinds of charges. If you get through a tax cycle and you notice that you have some penalties and interest because you didn't make those payments, you can file what's called Form 2210.[6] If you are over age sixty-two and you file this form, it can give you a "once-in-a-lifetime" abatement of the penalty and interest. If you are in this age bracket, review your 1040 from this past year. If you see any penalties, I encourage you to take advantage of Form 2210.

PART TWO

TAXES
AND
SOCIAL SECURITY

5

Don't Let Uncle Sam Steal Your Social Security Check

One thing is very true these days: your Social Security claiming strategy is critical as a pillar in your retirement planning. These are the dollars that you've been paying into the system for years, and I want you to wring every nickel out of the system when it comes time for you to claim Social Security.

Over the years, I've talked with clients about several strategies regarding how to maximize Social Security dollars. You've been paying into your retirement fund your whole working life. You've earned this, but there are ways to make sure you are getting the greatest benefit.

One strategy that is highly underutilized is called *voluntary suspension*. When you turn sixty-two, you are eligible to take Social Security. If you take it early at sixty-two, you will see a reduction in your benefit.

Unlock the power of "voluntary suspension"—
a little-known strategy that can let you collect
Social Security benefits early and
still maximize your payments later in life.

How does voluntary suspension play out? Let's assume you took the benefit early and have turned sixty-six or sixty-seven (it depends on your birth year) and are then eligible for full retirement. At that point in time, you can voluntarily suspend your benefit. From then on, it begins growing deferred at 8 percent per year. You can continue voluntary suspension up to age seventy.[7] This allows you to get money out of the system in your early sixties and then potentially suspend it and let it recoup much of the value left on the table at age sixty-two. This is especially helpful for situations where one spouse retires sooner and income needs to be supplemented.

One thing to note is that if you start receiving Social Security at age sixty-two and you want to turn it off the following year, you must pay back every dollar you collected. That's a tough check to write to the Social Security Administration, but when you take it early and you wait until your full retirement age, at that point you can suspend it and not have to pay back anything, and then it grows at 8 percent per year. With Social Security as the backbone of most Americans' retirement plans, this is a powerful strategy. For more strategies and a playbook for making decisions around Social Security, use the QR code below for access to the REAP Financial *Social Security Decision Guide.*

6

Tax-Free Social Security
How To Keep Every Penny

Even with all my years of retirement planning, I am still surprised when clients don't understand that Social Security benefits are taxable. Wasn't that money already taxed? While Federal Insurance Contribution Act (FICA) withholdings are a payroll tax, in exchange, you receive Social Security credit. When this money comes to you as income in retirement, it can be taxed as such.

Is that the end of the story? Is it possible to retire and not pay taxes on Social Security in today's America? The answer is absolutely. I'm going to show you how.

Yes, tax-free Social Security is possible.
The key isn't how much you have, but
where your income comes from in retirement.

Social Security may be taxable. The question is, how much tax do you have to pay? Unless you keep your income under very low limits, more than likely you will pay tax on your Social Security, and you'll be taxed at whatever your marginal bracket is each year. Up to 85 percent of your Social Security benefits can be taxed, but 85 percent of the benefit amount could be taxed at the marginal bracket. Sometimes when people hear 85 percent, they imagine an 85 percent tax, but that is not the case.

Prior to 1983, Social Security was not taxed. Since then, your Social Security can remain untaxed if your income stays below a certain threshold: If you're a single filer and you make under $25,000 a year, or if you're a married filer and you make under $32,000 a year joint income, you don't have to pay tax on your Social Security. However, once you cross those thresholds, you start paying tax on your Social Security. Since 1983, those numbers have never been adjusted for inflation. This is how the government does it, right? It's stealthy, so you have to pay attention.

What income counts toward that income limit? It could be a pension. It could be rental income. Part-time work would count. Savvy investors like municipal bonds because the dividends and the interest are tax-free. Yet even that income counts toward those low-threshold income totals for Social Security.

Surely your Social Security check doesn't count, right? Actually, half of it does. The IRS counts half of whatever your Social Security benefit is toward the income limit. So, if you're a married couple, and let's say you have $2,000 each in Social Security, that's $48,000. Half of that is $24,000, which will count toward a $32,000 limit. It's almost impossible.

Here's how families we consult with can take Social Security early and stay under those limits. They've saved in a very tax-diversified way. If you can save in a tax-diversified way, you may be able to avoid paying taxes on Social Security because you're living on assets that are not counted at the bottom line of your 1040. This could be brokerage money, maybe it's a stockpile of cash, maybe it's Roth IRAs or health savings accounts. When you couple this with the voluntary suspension strategy from the last section, the impact on long-term retirement is massive.

Smart asset location is the secret.
By living on tax-free sources of money,
you can legally "look poor" on paper
and keep 100% of your Social Security check.

Why? Because the more you can keep out of the government's bank account via Social Security, the less you'll have to pull out of your assets, particularly early in retirement. The money gets to stay in your accounts, breaking a sweat working for you.

If this sounds good to you and you want to learn more, you can access the *Social Security Decision Guide* mentioned in the last chapter via the QR code below. It's ten-plus pages where we're going to dive into this and a lot more about strategies when it comes to what could be the pillar of your retirement.

This is your money. We want to wring every nickel out of it that we can.

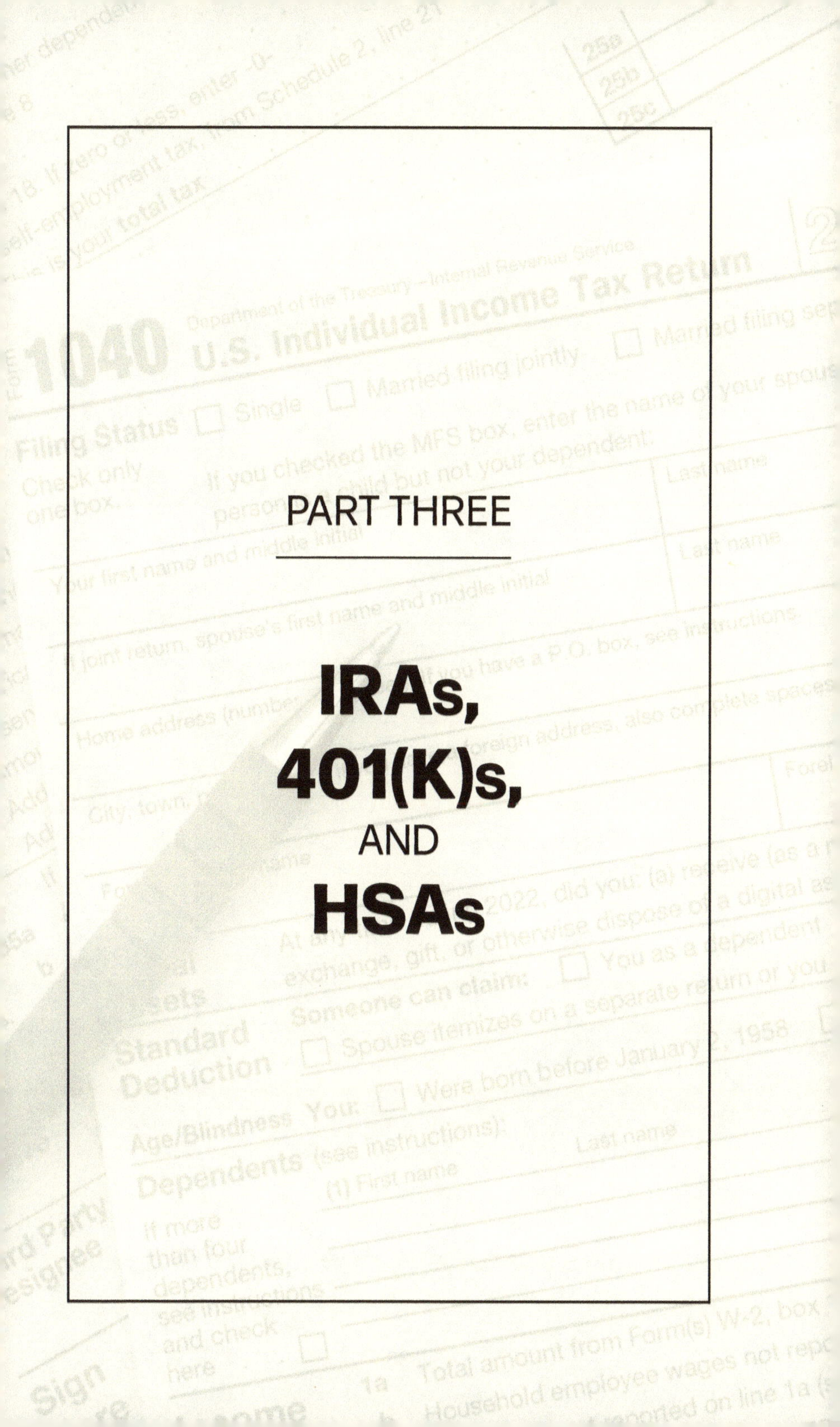

PART THREE

IRAs, 401(K)s, AND HSAs

7

Key Tips For Starting A Roth 401(k) And Roth IRA

For years, I've talked about the power of tax-free investing. Roth products provide a very accessible path to tax-free investing. Some of my favorite accounts I encourage clients to have in their portfolio are the Roth 401(k) and the Roth IRA. However, there are some key differences that you really need to understand to maximize the ability to grow your portfolio tax-free.

Contribution And Income Limits

The first difference between the two is contribution limits. Obviously, you must have earned income to contribute to an IRA and a 401(k), so that's the first criteria, but there are big differences in how much you can put into these accounts annually.

If you are under age fifty, you can, as of this writing, contribute $7,500 into a Roth IRA; if you have a Roth 401(k), you can contribute up to $24,500. If you are over age fifty and have a Roth IRA, you can contribute $8,600. They call that a *catch-up contribution*. If you are over fifty and have a Roth 401(k), you can contribute up to $32,500. Note: Always research to see what the numbers are in your current tax year.

What if you have both a Roth IRA and a Roth 401(k)? Can you put money into both? The answer for most of you is yes. You can contribute to a Roth IRA if your modified adjusted gross income (MAGI) is less than $153,000 as a single filer or less than $242,000 as a married couple filing jointly. The ability to contribute is reduced if your MAGI is between $153,000 and $168,000 (single) or $242,000 and $252,000 (jointly). You cannot contribute at all if your MAGI is $168,000 or more (single) or $252,000 or more (jointly). (Note: The IRS sets these income thresholds and they are subject to change annually.) This is where the Roth 401(k) becomes very useful. There are no income limits when it comes to a Roth 401(k).

Don't let income limits stop you.
The Roth 401(k) has no income cap,
making it a powerful tool for high earners
to build a tax-free nest egg.

Roth Conversions

What if you still have traditional IRAs and 401(k)s? The good news: It's not too late to do a Roth conversion. You can even do what's called a *backdoor Roth IRA conversion*. If you are over the income limits mentioned above, you can't contribute to a Roth IRA. What you can do is convert other IRA accounts into Roth IRA accounts.[8]

If you're invested in a Roth IRA, in most cases, you can invest that money in an array of things. It could be stocks, mutual funds, or exchange-traded funds (ETFs). Many folks are choosing to use self-directed IRAs to invest in tangible assets like real estate and gold. The list goes on.

In many cases, you might have a 401(k), maybe with an employer you used to work for. This is why a lot of people do 401(k) rollovers. They can move their 401(k) dollars that can only be held in the investments available there and become better diversified in many cases by rolling to either a Roth IRA or a traditional IRA.

(Not) Borrowing From A Roth

Many people choose to borrow money from their 401(k). Most companies will allow for 401(k) loans, so you can borrow from them and then pay them back over the years through payroll deductions. With a Roth IRA, a loan is not possible. There's no exception to that.

> With a Roth, you are in complete control. Your money can grow tax-free for your entire life, with no government-mandated withdrawals.

What about RMDs (required minimum distributions)? That's the power of Roth IRAs. There are no required minimum distributions on Roth IRAs. Prior to 2024, if you were of RMD age, you were forced to take the required minimum distributions on your Roth 401(k)s. The good news is you are no longer subject to the required minimum distribution on your Roth 401(k)s. Both Roth IRAs and Roth 401(k)s are now RMD-free, which is very powerful.

A Roth is a great tool to accumulate wealth, distribute it tax-free in retirement, and leave it to heirs tax-free.

8

Supercharge Your Roth IRA Growth

For years, we've consulted with families about the benefits of Roth IRAs and Roth 401(k)s. Many feel they are late to the game. If you are feeling that way, I want to share a little-known way to maximize your Roth very, very quickly.

Some see the tremendous tax-free benefits of a Roth IRA and Roth 401(k) but don't want to pay the price of admission. What's the price of admission? Typically, when you put money into a Roth, you don't get a tax deduction. However, what if there was a way to optimize your Roth savings?

There is, and it starts with an employer 401(k). You have probably been contributing to it for years, and if you're over age fifty, under today's law, you can max out contributions at $32,500, including a catch-up limit.

For those of you doing that, I commend you, but you don't have to stop there. As you approach retirement, in your fifties or early sixties, your situation is changing. You may have an empty nest. The kids are off the payroll, and you're hammering your savings. Excellent. To get maximum benefit from these savings, many employers offer after-tax contributions.

Supercharge your retirement with after-tax 401(k) contributions—a powerful strategy to funnel tens of thousands more into a Roth IRA each year.

What this means is that you can max out your traditional 401(k) or your Roth 401(k), and then you can put in additional dollars above and beyond that $32,500 limit. Under today's law, you can put up to $72,000 into a traditional 401(k) or Roth 401(k) plan.

Here's an example: Let's say you are contributing to your 401(k) at work. If you're over age fifty, you're putting $32,500 into your traditional 401(k). You're getting a tax deduction on that contribution. That is income not showing up on the bottom line. Then, if you choose, you can contribute an additional $39,500, which amounts to a total of $72,000. To be clear, that $39,500 is not tax-deductible. It still shows up as income. Why would you do that?

Obviously, you want to save for your future retirement, but this is where it gets interesting. Those dollars are designated as after-tax contributions upon retirement. Let's assume you've been doing that for many years. You can roll over the after-tax contribution amount that you've been putting in over the years into a Roth IRA.

Combine a Roth 401(k) with after-tax contributions to build a fortress of tax-free wealth for yourself and your heirs.

Think about it like a mega Roth conversion. This allows you to front-load your Roth IRAs upon retirement. If you've been putting money into Roth 401(k)s, that's something that's readily available at most employers today. Believe it or not, that money can be rolled into a Roth IRA as well, with no taxes. Assuming you're doing the Roth 401(k) and the after-tax contributions, you could find yourself walking into retirement with a substantial amount of forever tax-free wealth that could also be left to your heirs tax-free.

Most importantly, when it becomes the money you live on, it will never show up as income. The bottom line is income. You are in control of your Roth dollars. There are no RMDs on Roth IRAs. It's a powerful account and one that's heavily underutilized. This strategy can really help you get a jump start in the Roth arena. Check with your employer, see if that's an option for you, and consider your savings plan and your tax-free retirement income.

For those of you in the "retirement red zone" specifically ages sixty, sixty-one, sixty-two, and sixty-three, the government has handed you a golden ticket. In 2026, the catch-up contribution limit for this specific age group increases significantly. Instead of the standard catch-up (projected at $8,000), you are eligible for a "Super Catch-Up" of $11,250.

This means that if you max out your standard deferral ($24,500) plus this special catch-up, you could contribute $35,750 to your 401(k) in a single year. However, there is a critical twist for high earners: If your FICA wages from your employer exceeded $150,000 (indexed for inflation) in the prior year, Uncle Sam mandates that this catch-up contribution be made to a Roth 401(k). You pay tax now, but lock in tax-free growth forever. A "forced" benefit that aligns perfectly with our strategy to disinherit Uncle Sam.

9

Avoiding Tax Traps On The Road To Retirement

You are driving along, minding your own business, cruising a few miles above the speed limit—it was 55 mph the last time you checked—when you suddenly see flashing lights in the rearview mirror. You look up, and there it is, a sign marked "Speed Limit 35 mph." It's a classic speed trap. When there are police hidden behind the next curve in the road, your GPS even alerts you: speed trap ahead.

Similarly, there are four retirement tax traps that can derail your retirement. Fortunately, there are ways to avoid these types of pitfalls. When we look at a retirement plan, we often focus on an income planning portfolio that will grow enough to maintain our standard of living and outlast us. That's the hope, right? However, there are some often overlooked tax situations that can make a drastic impact on your spending and the longevity of your portfolio.

Tax Trap Number One: Net Investment Income Tax (NIIT)

A significant tax trap is the Net Investment Income Tax (NIIT), which is an additional 3.8 percent tax on investment income for higher earners.[9] The crucial detail is that while the tax is applied specifically to your investment income, it is your total income that determines if you are subject to it. The NIIT applies when your Modified Adjusted Gross Income (MAGI)—which includes wages, business income, and investments—exceeds $200,000 for single filers or $250,000 for married couples filing jointly. Once you cross that threshold, the 3.8 percent tax is calculated on the **lesser** of either your total net investment income or the amount your MAGI is over the limit.

You may have a single year where you've got capital gains or, for whatever reason, an increase in income for that year. By understanding your income today and then projecting ten, twenty, or thirty years out, you will be in a better position to make changes to accommodate the NIIT.

It sounds minimal. A 3.8 percent tax doesn't sound like a lot, but it can add up over many years. That additional 3.8 percent can really take a toll in the long term. It's a lot of money going back to the government.

You may be thinking, "I won't be in a $250,000 income range in retirement." The primary factor that really contributes to this issue is when your IRA or 401(k) required distribution kicks in. You may find you have a very large required distribution that will push you into higher tax brackets.

Beware the 3.8 percent Net Investment Income Tax. Your future RMDs could easily push you over the income threshold, triggering this costly surtax.

Here's the thing: If you did a great job of saving in your IRAs and 401(k)s, you are facing potentially huge required minimum distributions (RMDs) down the road. It is not uncommon for families to have $100,000, $150,000, or more in RMDs. Add to that your Social Security income and other sources like pension or rental properties, and guess what? You can find yourself over those limits. This not only puts you in higher tax brackets in retirement, but you're also paying NIIT.

Tax Trap Number Two: Social Security

Most people don't understand that you will likely pay taxes on your Social Security. It's very hard not to. Let's rewind the clock back to 1983. As I mentioned previously, that's when taxes began showing up on retirees' Social Security payments, and the federal government put income limits on Social Security. If you could keep your income under those limits, you didn't pay any tax. Shockingly, those limits from 1983—forty years ago—have never gone up, but here's the catch: everything else has, including your Social Security check. So, all this time later, you still need to keep income under $25,000 a year as a single filer so as not to pay tax on Social Security.

The income limits for taxing Social Security benefits are stuck in 1983. That's why for most retirees today, paying tax on Social Security is almost unavoidable—unless you have a plan.

For that reason, over 80 percent of Americans pay tax on Social Security. Practically speaking, you almost have to be at the poverty level to avoid paying tax on Social Security. If you're married, you have to have an under $32,000 modified adjusted gross income (MAGI) to pay 0 percent tax on your Social Security. If you have $44,000 in MAGI or less, only 50 percent of your Social Security is taxable.

Now, get this: If you earn anything over $44,000 as a married couple, 85 percent of your Social Security will be taxed. This is another weird quirk of the tax system. You don't get taxed on 100 percent of the Social Security income. Note: This is *not* an 85 percent tax; 85 percent of your benefit will be taxed at your marginal bracket. As you plan for your retirement, when you see that little number on the corner of your Social Security statement, the benefit amount that you've been paying into for years, that's likely not the number you will net after tax. It's likely to be much smaller than that.

Tax Trap Number Three: Medicare

One of the big reasons you need an income plan in retirement is to avoid overpaying for Medicare.

There are five different premium payment tiers. An average recipient may pay in the neighborhood of $350 to $375 on Medicare A, B, D, and supplemental per month per person. Would it shock you to know that we have families paying well over $600 per person for the same Medicare coverage their neighbors are getting? That's true. It's because the Medicare premiums are dictated by your income. For married couples, if you make over $218,000, your Medicare premium will start increasing.

That is why another trap to avoid, if possible, concerns Medicare premiums and income-related monthly adjustment amounts (IRMAAs). The IRMAA is a Medicare surtax. I call it a stealth tax. Again, income level dictates whether or not you pay more in Medicare. In 2026, if you are married and make $218,000 or less or are single and make $109,000 or less during the year, you will not be assessed the IRMAA surcharge.[10]

Be aware that your income needs will likely rise over time due to inflation. This can push you over these thresholds as you withdraw more from your portfolio and receive cost-of-living adjustments on Social Security. You may sell a highly appreciated home or something and be above those limits. IRMAA charges can take a great toll. We see families that pay hundreds of thousands of dollars more on their Medicare premiums over the course of their retirement.

Working with your tax planner or investment advisor on an income plan to stay below the current Medicare maximums for income will help you avoid this scenario.

Tax Trap Number Four: What You Leave To Beneficiaries

In recent years, Congress passed what is known as the SECURE Act 2.0. The SECURE Act 2.0 changed the game in a lot of positive ways for retirees, but it also changed the game in some not-so-positive ways for your beneficiaries—your kids, the people, and the families that are going to inherit your wealth. Under the new law, they now require the inheritor of an IRA or a 401(k) to take that money out of the account within ten years. Isn't inheriting wealth a good problem? Yes, but we want to make sure you don't grossly overpay in taxes.

Before the SECURE Act 2.0 passed, when you inherited an IRA, you could place it into what is called a *stretch IRA*, and you may have had to withdraw a small amount every year, but most of that money could continue to grow, and it really didn't make an impact.

The SECURE Act turned inherited IRAs
into a potential "tax bomb" for your children,
forcing them to withdraw—and pay taxes on—
the entire account within 10 years.

Now, if you inherit an IRA worth a million dollars today and are forced to take that money out over ten years, 100 percent of that money in a traditional IRA or traditional 401(k) is 100 percent taxable. So, when you pass away in your eighties or nineties, your children could be in their fifties, sixties, or seventies—their highest earning years. They will now inherit your pretax IRAs and have to pull significant amounts of money out, potentially at very high tax rates.

Here's the thing: There are ways to potentially keep more of your wealth. Use the QR code below to access our updated *SECURE Act 2.0* report and learn the pros and cons that have come with this legislation.

10

You've Saved A Fortune
Now Protect It

Many high earners believe they don't have much, if anything, to gain from a Roth IRA. Nonsense! The Roth IRA is one of the most efficient vehicles in the tax code. High earners may think they make too much money to qualify for a Roth. That may or may not be true. Here's why.

Currently, if you're a single tax filer making under $153,000, or married and earning under $242,000, you are still eligible for the Roth game. As you begin earning over these thresholds, you get phased out. So, game over, right?

> A Roth conversion is a surgical strike,
> not a carpet bomb. Convert strategically
> to fill up your current tax bracket
> without spilling over into a higher one.

Not so fast. There are income limits on contributions. However, refer back to chapter 7, where I explain how a Roth conversion works. This is not new money. In fact, if you have a single dollar in a traditional IRA or 401(k), you can convert to a Roth. No matter what your age or income, you can take money in these accounts—pretax IRAs or 401(k)s—and convert it in the same year to a Roth IRA. Be careful; every dollar you convert will show up on the bottom line of your 1040. If you convert too much in a given year, you could push yourself into a higher tax bracket.

For perspective on how most Americans save, consider the following data from the Federal Reserve.

Average Retirement Savings Balance By Age

Perhaps the most official measure of American retirement savings comes from the Federal Reserve System. The Fed calculated average retirement account balances for individuals as of 2022, the latest year for which figures are available. Broken down by age, those balances are as follows:

Age	Average Retirement Account Balance
Younger than 35	$49,130
35–44	$141,520
45–54	$313,220
55–64	$537,560
65–74	$609,230
75 or older	$462,410

Of course, averages can be skewed by those who have large nest eggs, and median numbers are significantly lower, according to the Federal Reserve. For instance, the median savings of those aged 35 to 44 is $45,000. The median is the number at which half the people in a group have saved more and half have saved less.

Federal Reserve Board's Survey of Consumer Finances.[11, 12]

A very sensible way to go about it would be to look at your tax bracket this year. How much headroom do you have as far as the income you're making, and what is the very top of your current bracket? Now, you can convert enough to stay in the same tax bracket this year. As always, consult with a CPA or a tax attorney prior to doing this, but I want you to know you can get in the Roth game.

***

Pay tax on the "seed" today, not the "harvest" tomorrow. A Roth conversion is a calculated move to secure a lifetime of tax-free growth.

***

Most Americans have the bulk of their retirement funds in an IRA or 401(k). Why? We like tax deductions. When you put money into a Roth IRA, you don't get a tax deduction. However, remember that money in a traditional IRA or 401(k) is tax-deferred, not tax-free. When you convert money to a Roth IRA, it creates a tax, but never forget that the money will then grow tax-free forever.

Think about this: Tax rates are currently at their lowest point in decades. Taxes are on sale right now, and if you're like me, you know they will go up, and they'll probably never be this low again in our lifetime. Now is a golden opportunity to consider taking dollars in IRAs and 401(k)s and potentially converting them to Roth IRAs at record-low tax rates because the dollars in your IRA and 401(k) continue to grow for years to come.

When you live on these retirement accounts, those dollars will count as income, and they could be counted as income at a time in the future when tax rates are exponentially higher than they are today. So, do you want to be taxed on the seed or the harvest? Everybody says the seed, but if the bulk of your wealth is in IRAs and 401(k)s, you're inadvertently setting yourself up to be taxed on the harvest.

Consider the impact of the 2017 Tax Cuts and Jobs Act (TCJA). Before this legislation, converting $200,000 from a traditional IRA to a Roth IRA would have cost the average individual roughly $56,000 in taxes. It was a steep price that required careful, often hesitant, planning. Today, the math has changed significantly. Under the current tax code, that same $200,000 conversion costs approximately $44,000—a $12,000 savings. While these lower rates were originally set to expire, the One Big Beautiful Bill Act (OBBBA) passed in July 2025 made these favorable brackets permanent. The looming threat of a 2026 tax hike is gone, locking in this window of opportunity for savers.

When you do that over a few more years at these record-low tax rates, the cumulative effect of that is $12,000 in savings each year over the next three years. That's $36,000 on the same conversion just because taxes are at historical lows.

11

The End Of Tax Deferral
What It Means For You

It was another meeting with a client who couldn't believe they were paying more in taxes during retirement. This was not unusual. Many retirees who work with me say, "Chris, if I just had known that I was going to be in the same tax bracket or higher, I would've changed where and how I saved." People assume that when their paycheck goes away, they will be in a lower tax bracket, but that's not the case for many successful retirees today.

For those of you who aren't yet retired, if you knew that you were going to be in a higher tax bracket in retirement, would that change the way you're saving and investing today? I want to show you why so many successful retirees find themselves in higher tax brackets when they retire—even if the tax rates stay as low as they are today.

The most dangerous myth in retirement planning? Believing your tax bracket will automatically drop. For successful savers, the opposite is often true.

The truth is, tax deferral, through IRAs and 401(k)s, may not be the best approach as you're heading into retirement. Of course, tax deferral is really the foundation of most people's savings and retirement plans. When they rolled out 401(k)s back in the '80s, the idea was that you could put money aside, your employer might match it, and it was not taxed at the time. Then you could take it out in retirement when the paycheck was gone and pay your taxes on it, again assuming you would be in a lower tax bracket.

That made a lot of sense, but I've been arguing about that for many years since the Roth IRA and now Roth 401(k) are available. The thing about tax deferral is that when you have money compounded in these accounts, it's a one-sided relationship. Uncle Sam dictates how much he will take.

Many people will defer the taxes in IRAs and 401(k)s until they're forced to take RMDs at age seventy-three. For example, the SECURE 2.0 Act of 2022 increased the RMD age from 72 to 73 for individuals who turn 72 after December 31, 2022. This applies to people born in the years 1951 through 1959. The law further pushes the RMD age to 75 for individuals who turn 74 after December 31, 2032. This applies to those born in 1960 or later.

In many cases, you see families go up in tax brackets because every dollar that comes out of their IRAs and 401(k)s is taxed at income rates, not the favorable capital gains rates, which are generally in the 15 to 20 percent tax range. As you approach your mid-seventies, you may be in a 12 percent or 22 percent tax bracket. If you have a sizable required distribution, now you're going from 12 percent to 22 percent or 24 percent to 32 percent. What that means is that every dollar now forced to come out of those IRAs and 401(k)s will be taxed at higher rates, in many cases indefinitely.

As noted in previous chapters, it also means that your Social Security will be taxed at higher rates. You could potentially have pension income, stealth taxes on Medicare, and taxes on inherited IRAs and 401(k)s. The point is, these tax-deferred accounts have some significant downside for today's retirees.

Another reason to say goodbye to tax deferral is that when you lose a spouse in late life, in many cases, your portfolio shrinks overnight because you are now filing taxes as a single filer. When you inherit or receive your spouse's IRA or 401(k), you will still be required to take the required minimum distribution on that, but now you're filing at single taxpayer rates, which are very unfavorable. I call this the widow(er)'s penalty, like we discussed previously. In many cases, you see your tax bracket and your Medicare premiums go up because you don't have that favorable filing joint bracket. These are just a few reasons to consider the Roth IRA. If you're still working, consider putting money into Roth 401(k)s. These are powerful ways to build a foundation of tax-free money for both you and your heirs.

Roth accounts are a powerful defense
against the "widow(er)'s penalty."
They protect the surviving spouse from
a sudden, massive tax increase.

The most important thing is that these Roth products give you more control because, currently, they aren't subject to required minimum distributions. That's why you want to have these Roth accounts in your portfolio. If the majority of your portfolio is in pretax accounts, like most Americans, and you want to get in the Roth environment, use the QR code below to get your hands on our *Tax Explorer Guide.*

12

Master The Art Of Timing
When To Convert Your IRA

Many families are becoming aware of how powerful Roth IRAs and Roth conversions can be in their long-term retirement planning, but you may be making too much money to contribute to a Roth IRA.[13] In chapter 10, I showed how it is possible to convert to a Roth despite income caps. In this chapter, I share a strategy to determine the timing of those conversions.

Here's a refresher on the basic income thresholds for a Roth IRA. If you are currently working and are a single filer and make over $153,000 (MAGI), or if you're a married couple and you make over $242,000 in modified adjusted gross income, the IRS says you cannot put money directly into a Roth IRA. However, as the saying goes, timing is everything.

I briefly discussed the backdoor Roth conversion, but it's an underutilized strategy that deserves a closer look. Here's a more detailed explanation of how it can be used: This strategy allows you to put money directly into your traditional IRA. Because you're making over those income limits, you can add money to your IRA, but there will not be a tax deduction. It's called a *nondeductible IRA contribution*. What you can then do in the same year is convert the amount you contributed to a Roth IRA. That's the backdoor strategy. I don't know why the IRS makes us do it this way, but it's something that's been around for a long time, and the strategy's validity should always be checked with a CPA.

Is this strategy for you? Before you try it, always consult with a CPA for two reasons. Number one, when you convert, in some cases, it can be a taxable event. Now, this strategy of the backdoor doesn't necessarily mean that it's going to be a taxable conversion, but whether you have a single dollar or hundreds of millions of dollars in IRAs, there's something called a *pro-rata rule* that could make a partial amount or even the full amount taxable. This is because the IRS considers all of your traditional IRAs as one large account. If you have other IRAs with pre-tax money, a portion of your backdoor conversion will be taxed. I also want you to consult with your CPA or accountant about whether or not the strategy is still available.

With tax rates at historic lows, the window
of opportunity for strategic Roth conversions
is wide open. This is the time to act.

This is a great strategy to consider for long-term tax control and tax savings. Remember, why do we pay the price of admission to get money in a Roth IRA? Because the day you get those dollars into a Roth IRA under today's law, that money will start growing forever tax-free.

Imagine the IRA or the 401(k) you have currently. Imagine if that money were growing tax-free right now. If it's a traditional IRA or 401(k), it's growing tax-deferred, but you will have to pay taxes someday when that money comes out. As those accounts continue to grow, you're setting yourself up to inadvertently be taxed on a bigger number. Not to mention, at this time, tax rates are as low as they have been in decades. It could be a terrific time for you to consider the Roth IRA, potentially even the backdoor Roth conversion.

When Should You Convert To A Roth?

Questions that we get all the time from successful investors and retirees are, "When is the best time to do a Roth conversion? Is it in this up market? Is it in a down market?" The markets have been all over the place the last couple of years. I want to fill you in on the silver lining of market volatility when it comes to your Roth conversions.

For a moment, think about a down stock market. Nobody likes 'em, but they happen, but there is a silver lining with a volatile stock market: You can do a Roth conversion at a discount when the markets are down. It's like Roth conversions are on sale.

A down market puts Roth conversions on sale. Converting when your account value is lower means paying less tax to secure a future of tax-free growth.

Why is this? Let's say you have $100,000 in the market, and the market is doing great. The account is worth a hundred grand, and you're thinking, "Hey, I'm going to convert it this year. That way, the money can forever grow for me tax-free." Well, that's a great idea. Everybody likes tax-free. In contrast, in a down market, let's say that $100,000 is now worth $70,000; it's down 30 percent. You haven't sold the shares. When you do a Roth conversion, you don't have to sell the shares either. You can convert the shares in-kind. You can convert that to $70,000. When the market comes back, you still own the same shares, and all of that growth back up to $100,000 and beyond is tax-free forever. By converting when values are lower, the taxes due are on that lower current value, allowing for significant future tax-free growth.

Not only is it tax-free for you, but your money is off the government plan. It will never be subject to the required minimum distribution. Plus, if you care to, you can leave that money to your heirs. So, I like Roth conversions, but our financial philosophy is to never pay a dollar more in tax than is legally required. So if you are going to have to pay taxes on a conversion, do it when taxes are on sale.

There's no limit on how much you convert, but be careful. You don't want to do too much. You don't want to push yourself into a bracket that you don't need to find yourself in. However, work with a trusted fiduciary advisor and consult your CPA, to determine how much you should convert to take advantage of these volatile markets, all the while at forty-year low tax brackets.

13

IRA-To-HSA Transfers
A Hidden Retirement Gem

Health savings accounts (HSAs) are a uniquely powerful wealth-building tool. They're highly underutilized, and you may be wondering how to fund them. There are some little-known strategies for funding this account directly from your IRA.

Now, a lot of people don't get excited about HSAs because you are pulling hard-earned money out of a paycheck into an account that can only be used for medical expenses. If you're young or even in your mid-years, you may not have a lot of medical expenses, so you don't really feel like you're saving for your future retirement. I get it. Hang in there with me, and I promise you will see why I am such a big fan.

If you have a high-deductible health insurance plan, chances are you qualify for an HSA. You may have an HSA through an employer, or you may just take advantage of one outside the employer. Currently, if you're a single filer, you can contribute up to $4,400 this year. If you have a married plan or a family plan, the limit is $8,750. If you are over age fifty-five, you can make a catch-up contribution of $1,000 above those limits.

Your Health Savings Account isn't just for doctor bills. It's a "super Roth"— a triple-tax-advantaged vehicle for generating tax-free retirement income.

An HSA has several benefits: First, when you put money into the account, you get a tax deduction. The money will grow tax-deferred through the years, and if it's used for qualified medical expenses, it comes out tax-free.

The second benefit is that, along the way, this money can be invested and can grow. This becomes part of a larger income strategy, using the money in your HSA account as tax-free retirement income down the road. How is this done? By keeping track of qualified medical expenses along the way, you can then cut yourself a retroactive reimbursement check. You could do this one time or with multiple distributions.

Another little-known method is that you can fund your HSA with your IRA.[14] With money in your IRA that you've already taken a tax deduction on, you could do a single, once-in-a-lifetime transfer from the IRA for the annual HSA maximum for a given year. This is a powerful strategy for those who are getting close to retirement and are looking for ways to get more control of tax liabilities.

> The HSA is the ultimate retirement tool:
> get a tax deduction now, enjoy tax-free growth,
> and withdraw your money tax-free later.

This can be a great way to fund your HSA in the final years of your working career. I want to be clear: Even if you have multiple IRAs, this is a once-in-a-lifetime opportunity. I encourage you to consult with your CPA or a fiduciary advisor on how to take advantage of this. If you have access to a health savings account, it's one of the most powerful retirement planning tools on the planet. We call it a super Roth. To reiterate, you get the tax deduction on the front, and you get the tax-free benefit on the back. This is one additional way to get an extra annual contribution with money that you've already set aside for your future retirement.

14

HSAs: The Secret To Building A Legacy

n the previous chapter, I walked you through the benefits an HSA provides you in the form of tax breaks and a source of retirement income. Now, I want to show you the power of the HSA and its legacy benefits.

The first rule of maximizing your HSA: don't use it. Pay for medical expenses out-of-pocket and let your HSA funds grow tax-free for decades.

Let me paint the picture for you. You establish a health savings account, and you can put generous amounts into these accounts as a family plan—well over $8,000 a year, tax-deductible. The money goes in, and you can often pick the type of investments you want. When you or your spouse or a child have a medical expense, we advise that you don't touch the HSA—don't pull out the HSA debit card.

Instead, as I advised in the previous chapter, keep a spreadsheet or a shoebox with medical expenses to track while you're funding your account. Chapter 13 was all about funding your retirement with retroactive checks from that beautiful HSA. Now, if you've been funding this account for years at $8,000 plus a year, with the compounding effect of that in the stock market and beyond, you could have tens of thousands, if not hundreds of thousands of dollars in the HSA by the time you retire. When it's time to live on the portfolio because the paycheck stops in retirement, you have a tax-free bucket of money, because you can reimburse yourself from that account. After age sixty-five, funds can be withdrawn for any reason without penalty, but will be taxed as ordinary income if not used for qualified medical expenses.

Here's a key detail to remember: If you had a $200,000 HSA and you had $120,000 in medical expenses along the way, well, you can only reimburse yourself for up to the $120,000. What happens to that $80,000 when you can't just reimburse it all out? Two options I like to present to clients are using a living trust or leaving the HSA to charitable causes you believe in.

An HSA can be a powerful legacy tool.
Naming a charity as the beneficiary ensures
100 percent of the funds go to a cause you love,
completely tax-free.

Let's look at that first option. You can put your beneficiary or beneficiaries of this HSA into your living trust. You may even want to make your trust the beneficiary and not your kids. If your trust is the beneficiary, when those dollars are inherited from the trust and then potentially distributed to the kids, you can have your estate pay the taxes instead of your kids. If your kids are in their fifties or sixties when you pass away, they're probably in their highest earning years. When they inherit an HSA that was not their HSA, any dollars that come out of it will be taxable to them. However, if you make your trust the beneficiary, you could potentially have your estate pay the tax, let it go to your heirs tax-free, and not be a burden on them.

What about the HSA as a contribution to charity? When you do this, it is 100 percent tax-free. This becomes a way to enhance your charitable gifts and magnify the family's charitable giving.

If you are someone who gives annual gifts to your children, there is another possibility. Since you can give up to $19,000 per person per year to friends and family, you could take part of that gift and have it fund their health savings account.

They get a personal tax deduction on their return and get a gift at the same time. It's a powerful combination of tax efficiency. Additionally, who doesn't like free money from Mom and Dad?

You can use these tax-wise gifts to enhance not only your family by keeping wealth in the family, but also to give to the causes you care about.

PART FOUR

PROACTIVE TAX
AND
LEGACY PLANNING

15

How The Rich Use Home Equity To Preserve Wealth

Some of the most wealthy and successful retirees are leveraging the equity in the brick and mortar of their homes. When you think of a retiree accessing equity in their homes through a home equity line of credit, reverse mortgage, or reverse line of credit, you may imagine they are putting an addition on their home or paying off some debt. Maybe they don't have other means, and that's why they need to access the equity. However, for so many of the successful clients we work with, it's not for any of those reasons. They use it as a contingency.

For the savvy retiree, home equity isn't a last resort—it's a strategic buffer used to protect their investment portfolio from down markets.

Imagine two brothers who retired at the same time, in 1999, with the same amount in their portfolio: $1.2 million. In the first year of retirement, there was a positive return, but in the period from 2000 to 2019, there were six market corrections, meaning six periods in which the market ended in negative territory. Brother one takes $50,000 out of his portfolio each year, with that number going up annually to account for inflation. At the end of year one, he took his $50,000, and there was still plenty of money left in the account.

In 2000, we went through the dot-com bubble, and there were multiple years of negative returns before things started to pick back up. We started seeing returns for a few years after that, and then 2008 hit, followed by two smaller corrections in the intervening years. Brother one has continued taking out $50,000 a year throughout the entire time period of 1999 to 2019, and twenty years later, there is just a little over $35,000 left in the portfolio. Brother one's money is not outlasting him.

Brother two has set up a home equity line of credit, and it's sitting on the sidelines, not to be used unless there is a negative market year. The contingency strategy is that if the market ends the year negatively, the following year, instead of selling assets or equities in his portfolio, he will use the line of credit, which means he does not have to sell his equities in a down market or following a down year.

Brother two has the same $50,000 coming out of his portfolio every year, starting in 1999. He had the same return that year, and of course went through the same tech wreck during the dot-com bust. During the three years when the market was down, 2000, 2001, and 2002, brother two did not withdraw from his portfolio. He pulled from the line of credit, which means his assets stayed in his account; he was able to rebound, and his money was working for him on the market's way back up.

This isn't about taking on debt; it's about creating liquidity. A line of credit is your portfolio's "shock absorber" for volatile years.

Six times during the twenty-year period from 1999 to 2019, brother two went to the contingency: the home equity line of credit. Twenty years later, there is still over $900,000 in his portfolio, whereas brother one was left with only $35,000. We don't like debt generally—we're trying to get you to pay the house off, not have lines of credit—but this can be one of the most powerful ways to give yourself a contingency.

If you don't want to touch your home equity line of credit, you can pledge asset loans. In many cases, you pledge your brokerage portfolio and use that as collateral for a line of credit. There are several ways you can do this, but the question is, what is your contingency? You can see the impact of needing to pull from your portfolio in retirement during down-market years. It pays to have a contingency.

16

Unlocking Hidden Tax Benefits For Retirement

All of us are wired to be begrudging at best about paying taxes. I get it. Add to that stories we all hear about how the ultrawealthy and the superaffluent find ways to pay a lot less in taxes. What do they know that the rest of us don't? Read on and find out.

The heartbeat of this book is to help people find the tools to pay as little in taxes as possible in retirement. That's why I am so eager to share how the most successful retirees employ strategies to help protect their wealth from undue taxation. I love helping families implement these strategies, and believe it or not, you don't have to have tens or hundreds of millions of dollars to take advantage of these types of planning strategies.

Diversify Like The Ultrarich

Number one, consider unique investment products. A typical investment portfolio is composed of stocks, bonds, and maybe mutual funds on a retail investment scale. Most investors, as they're working through their careers and growing their net worth, are investing in mutual funds.

While mutual funds are a great tool for diversification, there are other types of investments, called *exchange-traded funds* (ETFs), that may be better. On an institutional level, where more wealthy families invest, mutual funds are not the go-to because there are a lot of hidden fees. There are management fees, commissions, and fees for entering and exiting a fund, so there's quite a bit of "gotcha" when it comes to mutual funds.

Beyond that, and what I really want people to understand, is that mutual funds can create a lot of tax inefficiency. You may be unaware of all the buying and selling going on in a given year related to your position in the fund, yet those gains and losses may show up on your tax return. To gain control of your taxes and keep more of your wealth, you want to know what's going on in your investments.

ETFs can be more tax-efficient. They are generally more affordable. There are also products called *buffered* ETFs, and many of our successful families utilize these. Buffered ETFs, as the name implies, allow you to be in the market and have downside protection. Let's say you have a 10 percent buffer on your ETF and the market falls 12 percent. In that case, you're only down 2 percent. To be clear, you are also limited on the upside. Let's say the market goes up by 15 percent; maybe you will make 10 percent of that. That's still not a shabby return.

There are many ways to invest and have downside protection. Consider investments beyond stocks and bonds. Maybe it's commodities, agriculture, energy, or metals like gold and silver mining. These things can provide that zig and zag of diversification in your portfolio.

Then there is real estate. Real estate has done really well. There are ways to do this as a retiree, where you don't have to take tenant calls about a broken water heater in the middle of the night. You can invest in real estate in passive ways that can really complement and bring stability to your portfolio.

Another tool that many successful families use is called a *multi-year guaranteed annuity*—MYGA.[15] The reason we like MYGAs today is that they're like CDs. They come in one-, three-, and five-year durations and longer. We typically stick in that three-to-five-year range. At the time of writing, you can find rates around 5 percent on a fixed rate MYGA for three, four, or five years in many cases.

True diversification means building a portfolio
that provides stability and peace of mind,
no matter what the stock market is doing.

The reason I like MYGAs is that they provide a guaranteed return. No matter what the stock market is doing, they grow tax-deferred, unlike a CD. You get a 1099 on that CD; on a MYGA, you don't. You can just sit back and let them compound. When it comes to the end of maturity, you can do what's called a 1035 exchange and transfer them to new MYGAs tax-free. A 1035 exchange is a provision in the US tax code that allows you to swap one insurance or annuity product for another of a "like kind" without triggering immediate tax consequences on the investment gains. This is beneficial when you want to move to a policy with better features, lower fees, or different benefits that better suit your current financial needs. To qualify, the exchange must be a direct transfer between the insurance companies, and you cannot personally receive the funds. The owner and insured on both the old and new policies must generally be the same to maintain the tax-deferred status. It's important to note that this strategy is most effective for non-qualified money (assets held outside of tax-advantaged retirement accounts like IRAs).

The benefit of a MYGA is that it grows tax-deferred, which allows you to 'look poor on paper' each year by not having to report the growth as current income. With guaranteed rates and protection of the principal, a MYGA offers stability. All of this diversification inside and outside the stock market gives retirees a level of confidence when the markets are jittery.

Find Tax Savings Like The Ultrarich

When you think about tax saving strategies, *where* you're saving money is just as important as *how much* you're saving. When we were growing up, our parents and grandparents always said to save until it hurts, and then save a little bit more. However, it's just as important to consider where you're saving, not just how much you're saving, because you have to consider how much of that money you are going to keep. This is what we covered in chapter 10.

Why does it matter where you are saving? If you have a 401(k) worth $2 million, that seems great. It's worth $2 million on paper, but after taxes, it is really worth about $1.5 million. If you've got traditional IRAs, they are all taxable as income. If you've got Roth IRAs, there's no tax when you withdraw. If you've got brokerage accounts, it's taxed at a favorable cap gains rate, maybe 15 percent or 20 percent. Your bank cash, your CDs, and money markets are taxed. It's 1099 income.

When looking at savings and investments, everyone looks at the gross number, but if you're like me, it's all about the net, the bottom line. Consider where your assets are going every month, every year.

Wealthy families also take advantage of many of the tips I've shared in previous chapters. They don't overpay on Social Security—they keep taxable income below limits that would put them in a higher tax bracket. Again, pay attention to net income, not gross income. In chapter 2, I described the *stealth tax*, where money from things like a Medicare premium goes back to the government.

Wealthy retirees proactively move money from tax-deferred accounts to tax-free havens like Roth IRAs and HSAs.

Lastly, we have all heard about investment diversification. Consider tax diversification. This is one of the most critical pieces of a successful plan because you're saving and living on this money in retirement. You want to keep as much as possible. The sooner you understand tax diversification, the better, because all the money you have in different accounts will typically be taxed differently. The most successful retirees generally have a lot of money in IRAs and 401(k)s, but they transfer them into health savings accounts or Roth IRAs to avoid RMDs and taxes.

To learn more, use the QR code below to access our new resource, *Tax Strategies for Retirement*.

17

The One Number That Will Define Your Retirement

When thinking about a successful retirement, many people focus on their net worth. You've been saving and investing for many years, and for most people, net worth is just an arbitrary number. Everybody's a little different, but the question is, do you know what the most important number is in retirement? It's not what you think.

I remember a meeting with a business owner who had just sold his company for $16 million. Good for him, right? He looked at me and said, "Chris, I need $60,000 a month to do what I want to do in retirement." I told him, "I've been doing this long enough to know you're going to be out of money in ten years." I came to find out that I was wrong: He ran out of money in twelve years. Pretty close.

The most important number in your retirement isn't your net worth—it's your annual budget. This single number determines the sustainability of your entire plan.

The point is, it's not about the amount you've saved; it's about the amount that's needed to maintain or even increase your lifestyle in retirement. Things like rate of return on investment are important, but what's even more important is having a plan to keep more wealth and pay fewer taxes. The more you can keep year after year, the more money you make by it breaking a sweat working and compounding for you, the better you maintain your portfolio.

You can have a number like my $60,000-a-month client, or $6,000 a month, or anywhere in between. Whatever it is, you need to know that number, and you need to have a plan to sustain it. When my team and I take successful retirees through this process, we see it over and over again: a few hundred dollars a month can make or break a plan.

How is that possible? Think of it this way: $300, $400, or $500 a month times a thirty-year retirement—that is a lot of money that draws down on the portfolio.

It all comes down to your withdrawal rate. Do you know what your withdrawal rate is right now? When you are retired, do you know what it will be? Your annual withdrawal rate really needs to be under 1 percent for that first decade of retirement if you're retiring in your early to mid-sixties. Having a budget is the most powerful thing for supporting your success in retirement.

Now, it doesn't sound fun, but I've made it easy for you. When you use the QR code below, you'll find the *REAP Financial Budget Worksheet*. It'll walk you through a preretirement and postretirement budget and make the process very simple.

18

Tax Diversification
The Key To A Secure Retirement

Now let's do a deep dive on a topic I discussed in chapter 16. One of the most overused words in the financial industry is *diversification*. You hear it all the time, but I want to talk about a different type of diversification, one that can make just as much, if not more, of an impact on your future retirement. It's called *tax diversification*, and it's the one way that you can get control of your income and get Uncle Sam disinherited from your wealth long term in retirement.

When I use the term *tax diversification*, it means saving in a certain way through your working career followed by a postretirement of positioning assets. This should be done in a way that will give you flexibility and control when it comes to your taxes. The myth is that when you retire, you will be in a lower tax bracket because the paycheck goes away, but for the successful families we consult with, often, that's not what happens.

The bulk of a family's wealth in America is saved in IRAs and 401(k)s. It's in a 403(b), or perhaps a 457(b). That's where the bulk of America's wealth has been saved, in these tax-deferred accounts. People do that over the years because they like tax deductions. American retirees are in desperate need of tax diversification.

The key to controlling your retirement is tax diversification—owning assets in taxable, tax-deferred, and tax-free buckets.

Money in retirement can be divided into several "tax buckets." The first bucket is *taxable money*. When you consider inflation as high as it has been the last couple of years, it's painful. When we think about our money at the bank, the banks aren't generally paying good interest rates. I've been known to say, "If you're heavy in the banks, you're losing money safely."

This is not just because of inflation; it's because of taxes. Think about this. If you have a 1 percent bank CD or a money market that's kicking off a little yield here and there, even if you don't touch that money throughout the year, at the end of the year, you get a 1099, and you're paying tax on the dime a month of interest the bank's been giving you, and on top of that you factor in the loss of inflation. For greater control in retirement of your tax bracket, you need to start by examining where you are paying taxes on money that you're not even using.

Many people are shocked at the taxes they are paying on money that is just sitting there. This is because of dividends that are being generated in your brokerage accounts, and maybe you're reinvesting those. It's also because of the banks. You have a nest egg there, and you're probably getting a little bit of interest.

Are you paying "phantom taxes" every year on interest and dividends you never even spend? It's time to take control.

What else is in the taxable bucket? If you sell highly appreciated stocks, you'll pay capital gains at maybe a 15 percent or 20 percent rate, but if you have dividends in your investments, which a lot of retirees do, some of those dividends may be taxed as ordinary dividends. Some may be taxed as qualified dividends.

We want qualified dividends. Why? *Qualified* means that income, whether you're taking it or not, is being taxed at capital gains rates. *Ordinary* dividends mean you're being taxed at your marginal income rates, which are generally higher. So, are there ways to reposition your portfolio so you can reduce the dividend income that shows up on lines 3a and 3b on your 1040? There probably are.

The second tax bucket is obviously our favorite one. It's the *tax-free bucket*, and it's not just Roth IRAs. If you put money into a Roth, you don't get the tax deduction today, but that money will forever grow tax-free. You could put a thousand dollars in there, and whether it grows to $10,000 or $100,000, it's all yours. You know by now that my favorite thing about a Roth IRA is that it's not subject to the required minimum distribution. It gives you control, plus you leave the Roth IRA to your heirs tax-free if that's a value of yours.

However, there's another account out there that's even more powerful than the Roth. It's the health savings account (HSA). We went over this in some detail in chapter 13, but let me highlight some key points. Why is it so powerful when you put money into an HSA? You get a tax deduction, unlike with a Roth IRA. The funds can be invested in most cases. Then, when you pull it out for qualified medical expenses, guess what? It can come out tax-free, not just what you put in, but all the growth. That's why it is sometimes called a super Roth: You get the tax deduction on the front end, and on the back, it comes out tax-free.

How do you turn your doctor's bills into tax-free retirement income? Put money in your HSA each year and get a tax deduction when you have a doctor's bill, a copay, a prescription expense, or a self-pay. Don't pull out the checkbook or the debit card on the HSA. Start a spreadsheet. Keep track of all your medical expenses. It could be for a couple of years or for decades when you retire. Then you will have amassed money that has been accruing interest in this HSA. You've had qualified medical expenses along the way. You tally those up, and, when it's time, you can cut yourself a retroactive reimbursement check tax-free for every medical expense you had. The tax-free bucket allows you to reduce your income in retirement.

Bucket number three is for the estate tax. You may not be concerned about this right now. Currently, the federal estate tax limits are very high. The federal estate tax exemption is scheduled to increase annually based on inflation. For example, in 2025 the exemption was set to rise over $14 million for individuals and over $28 million for married couples. The exemption is set to increase even more in 2026 to $15 million for individuals and $30 million for married couples.

With these high exemption amounts, most people do not worry about federal estate taxes. However, over the last two decades, the federal estate tax exemption has been a moving target in Washington, with the amount fluctuating based on the political climate. While the exemption is currently at a historic high, there have been serious legislative proposals, particularly from Democratic lawmakers, to significantly lower it to levels as modest as $3.5 million per individual. If that were to pass over the next twenty years, as your wealth continues to grow, this might be a concern you face.

An estate tax bucket could be where a family has assets that are earmarked for their heirs or causes they believe in. Those assets could potentially be in a life insurance policy, and that money then goes tax-free to the heirs. There are elaborate trusts that can be set up around properly structured life insurance policies as well, but this is money that, in many cases, families use to enhance their legacy, bequeath more, or set aside to pay for estate taxes. Keep an eye on that one, as the limits could be changing in the years to come.

If this is striking a chord and you want to see how to reposition assets, use the QR code below to get your hands on my report, *Tax Strategies for Retirement*, and see how tax buckets can give you choices and flexibility in retirement.

19

Disinherit Uncle Sam
Proactive Tax Planning Strategies

By now, it should be abundantly clear to you that one of the most powerful things a pre- and post-retiree can do in their retirement planning is proactive tax planning. No one wants to be forced into being reactive when they discover, in retirement, that taxes are a major factor in how long their financial reserves and other resources will last. A proactive tax plan will set you on a trajectory to keep exponentially more of your wealth, spend more of your wealth, and leave more to your heirs.

For many people, tax planning starts around mid-January, collecting documents—for everything from your brokerage accounts, bank accounts, and mortgage accounts—combining them, and sending them off to your CPA. The CPA then tells you what you owe or what you are getting back. For most people, that's where tax planning begins and ends.

Stop thinking about tax preparation and start thinking about tax planning. One looks backward at what you owe; the other looks forward at what you can save.

What does it look like to be more proactive? We get this question a lot. It has nothing to do with the CPAs out there. You need to understand that your CPA's job is mostly reporting your income history for the past year, not necessarily giving you proactive tax advice. You might email or call your CPA in late March asking, "What could I be doing to save on taxes?" That's the definition of reactive tax planning.

Proactive tax planning is looking beyond the tax cycle you're in today. It's looking at how you are likely to generate income in the most tax-efficient way long-term. It's looking at how you can grow your wealth over the next five, ten, twenty years, and beyond. It is about planning how you will withdraw that money in a way that will be taxed at the bare minimum.

Proactive tax planning is determining how you can keep Medicare premiums at the base and your Social Security taxation at the absolute minimum. It's also what I have been covering about how to pay fewer taxes on IRAs and 401(k)s and stay in a lower tax bracket.

I've referred to the "financial religion" of tax deferment we have been sold on. We're so focused on not paying tax today that we can miss grand opportunities right in front of us.

This is advanced tax planning for tax reduction, not tax avoidance. I don't mind paying my fair share, but no more. That's the mindset of the successful families who consult at REAP Financial. The goal is to work to avoid trading a small tax deduction today for significant taxes later on. The smarter move may potentially be to pay a little bit of tax today to ensure that a bigger number down the road is minimally taxed or even tax-free.

It boils down to saving in a tax-diversified way, giving you control long term, because if you do this correctly, you'll have more control over your taxes in retirement than at any time in your life. That is a true fact, and it's what we help our families do best.

20

Maximizing Your Legacy
Strategies For Generational Wealth

In this chapter, I want to focus on how to maximize your legacy, and by maximize it, I mean find ways to "disinherit" Uncle Sam from your investments and your wealth. This chapter is all about how to leave as much as you can tax-free to your heirs and magnify your charitable gifts.

Charitable Giving

If you have charitable intent, one of the most powerful accounts out there, and in my opinion, one of the most underutilized, is a *donor-advised fund*. This is for families that have charitable intent and can maybe give charitably on an annual basis.

In my financial consulting, I look at everything through the lens of tax saving. A donor-advised fund is a great idea, not just for legacy planning, but also for tax savings today and in future years. You can open a donor-advised fund and think about it like a charitable savings account. You can even donate to it stocks out of your brokerage account, cash, and a number of other assets and get a potentially sizable tax deduction in the process.

A donor-advised fund is your charitable savings account. It allows you to claim a large tax deduction today while giving to your favorite causes for years to come.

A key feature of a donor-advised fund is that it allows you to separate the timing of your tax deduction from your charitable giving. This is especially useful if you have a high-income year and want to maximize your tax benefits. For example, let's say you usually donate $10,000 to charity each year. In a year where you have a significant taxable event, like a stock sale or Roth conversion, you can contribute multiple years' worth of donations—say $50,000—into a donor-advised fund all at once. You get the $50,000 tax deduction in that high-income year, when it will have the most significant impact.

The money is now in a charitable investment account that you control. You can then grant that money to your favorite charities over the next five years or on whatever time frame you choose, all while benefiting from the large one-time tax deduction.

That's a beautiful thing with the donor-advised fund. You can donate the money, stocks, or whatever you choose, and that money can be invested in pretty much anything you would like it to be. Then, you can direct dollars out of your charitable savings account at any time throughout the year or multiple years to any charity of your choice.

In fact, you could even leave this to your heirs, and they could continue to give in the family name. If you want to take it a step further, you could even dictate in your trust how those funds have to be used while you're here and even when you're gone. It's a very powerful and underutilized tool.

Tax-Free Inheritance

There are a number of ways you can leave assets tax-free. This is, again, why the Roth IRA is one of our favorite accounts. Life insurance can be another vehicle for transferring wealth. Many of our successful families utilize life insurance, not because they need it, but because it is one of the most powerful ways to take a small number of dollars and turn it into what could be a meaningful death benefit. Life insurance, in most cases, goes 100 percent tax-free to your heirs.

For the affluent, life insurance isn't about income replacement—it's about wealth transfer. It's the most efficient tool for creating a large, tax-free legacy for your heirs.

One last note when it comes to designating beneficiaries for your accounts: If you've got IRAs and 401(k)s, those should be the first accounts you designate as charity beneficiaries. The reason is that if you leave the IRA or 401(k) traditional accounts to your kids, those dollars will be taxable to them. If you leave the accounts to a qualified charity, specifically, a nonprofit organization recognized by the IRS as a 501(c)(3), they receive the funds tax-free, meaning more of your dollars will make a lasting impact on the causes you believe in. A 501(c)(3) is a nonprofit organization that the Internal Revenue Service (IRS) has recognized as being tax-exempt. This status is granted to entities that are organized and operated exclusively for religious, charitable, scientific, literary, or educational purposes. A key benefit of this designation is that donations made to a 501(c)(3) organization are generally tax-deductible for the donor.

21

Preserving Wealth And Legacy
The Final Step To Retiring Rich And Looking Poor

As we approach the end of this journey, it's important to reflect on the ultimate goal: not just retiring rich, but ensuring that your wealth endures for generations to come. My firm, REAP Financial (www.reapfinancial.com), specializes in assisting families with their transition into retirement and beyond. In most cases, my clients have assets ranging from $2 million to $20 million. The most successful ones share one characteristic in common: They have a comprehensive estate plan in place.

The Importance Of Open Dialogue

One of the most important steps in preserving wealth is having open, honest conversations with your family. These discussions often involve tough questions—questions you may never have wanted to ask your parents or children. However, addressing these topics head-on is essential. If you're concerned about protecting your heirs and your legacy, don't wait until it's too late to start these conversations.

---

*Your legacy isn't built with documents alone;
it's built through conversation.
The most important estate planning you
can do starts at the family dinner table.*

Begin by asking yourself these two questions: "First, what do I want my money to accomplish while I'm here? Second, what legacy do I want to leave behind when I'm gone?" These questions aren't just about money; they're about aligning your goals and values with those of your spouse and heirs. For many business owners, wealth often comes in a lump sum during a capital event, such as selling a business. It's at this moment that many realize the importance of getting their financial house in order.

The Risks Of Second-Generation Wealth

Leaving a significant inheritance can be a double-edged sword. Without proper planning, the wealth you've worked hard to build can quickly diminish in the hands of the next generation. Money has a way of complicating relationships, even among the closest families.

Consider these questions: Who will manage the distribution of your wealth? Should your heirs receive their inheritance all at once, or over time?

In many cases, one child may be financially responsible, while another may struggle with spending. Tailoring your estate plan to reflect these differences is crucial. For example, you might choose to distribute wealth gradually over twenty years to a child who struggles with spending, while giving a more financially savvy heir access to their inheritance sooner.

The Role Of Stewardship

Second-generation wealth often lacks the stewardship that built it in the first place. Without guidance, heirs may mismanage their inheritance, spending or investing it recklessly. This is why it's so important to instill financial values in your heirs and ensure your estate plan reflects your wishes.

Navigating Tax Laws

Tax laws are constantly evolving, and what may not be an issue today could become one in the future. Families who don't believe they have an estate tax problem now may, in fact, face significant liabilities down the road. Forecasting your wealth over the next thirty years and planning accordingly is essential. The goal is to disinherit Uncle Sam, who could take up to 40 percent of your estate under current laws.

Understanding Your Family's Needs

The heart of our work is understanding our clients—not just their financial needs, but who they are as individuals. We use tools like personality assessments to better serve families and align them with the right strategies.

A truly successful financial plan is more than a collection of numbers— it's a reflection of your values, your history, and your hopes for the future.

For example, we often ask, "What's your greatest financial regret, and what has been your greatest accomplishment?" These questions reveal a lot about a person's values and priorities. Another powerful question we ask is, "If your parents were here today, would they be proud of you?" The answers often evoke deep emotions and provide insight into how our clients view their legacy.

Personality Types And Wealth Management

Through our work, we've identified several personality types that influence how people manage their wealth:

- *Family stewards*: They prioritize taking care of their families and relieving financial worries.

- *Independents*: They value personal freedom and see financial planning as a necessary evil.

- *Phobics*: They avoid complex decisions and prefer to delegate financial matters.

- *Anonymous*: They prioritize confidentiality and want their affairs handled discreetly.

- *Moguls*: They see wealth as a measure of success and seek control over their affairs.

- *VIPs*: They desire prestige and respect, often seeking high-status financial solutions.

- *Accumulators*: They focus on growing their wealth without spending it.

- *Gamblers*: They enjoy the thrill of financial problem-solving and complexity.

- *Innovators*: They view financial planning as an intellectual challenge and seek cutting-edge strategies.

Understanding these personalities helps us tailor our approach to each family's unique needs.

To help you discover your own financial personality, we've created the *Money Mastery Profile*—a simple, personalized assessment designed to reveal how you naturally approach money. Whether you are an accumulator focused on growth or a family steward focused on security, your profile offers valuable insight into how to build a retirement plan that aligns with your mindset.

Scan the QR code below to take the assessment in our *Money Mastery Profile*. It's quick, complimentary, and the first step toward a retirement strategy that's built around you.

The Final Takeaway

Retiring with substantial wealth is not a matter of chance. It is the product of disciplined planning, advanced tax and estate strategies, and an unwavering commitment to family values and generational stewardship. The real measure of success lies not just in the accumulation of assets, but in the sophistication with which those assets are preserved and transferred to future generations.

Those who thrive in retirement do so by fostering open, strategic dialogues within their families, building robust estate plans, and continuously adapting to ever-changing tax laws and economic realities. Strategic planning means proactively anticipating legislative changes, managing risks to second-generation wealth, and aligning every financial decision with deeply-held personal and family values. In these ways, your wealth becomes more than a number—it becomes a living reflection of your character and the legacy you wish to sustain.

The most important decision you will make is not only how to invest, but who you trust to guide your family's transition. At REAP Financial, the families we help create a road map for enduring prosperity are those who engage in rigorous, forward-thinking planning and surround themselves with a seasoned team of professionals who understand the intricacies of wealth, taxation, and legacy stewardship for portfolios ranging from $2 million to $20 million and beyond.

If you are serious about strategizing to preserve your life's work and ensuring your family flourishes for generations, now is the time to take meaningful action. The earlier you embark on comprehensive estate and tax planning, the more control, flexibility, and confidence you will have throughout retirement and beyond. This is the essence of "retiring rich and looking poor," leveraging advanced strategies to minimize unnecessary tax burdens while maximizing the impact and longevity of your legacy.

About The Author

Chris Heerlein is CEO of REAP Financial and the founder of REAP Private Client Group (RPCG), a dedicated wealth management practice. For over seventeen years, REAP Financial has served as a trusted architect of wealth for private business owners, corporate executives, and high-net-worth families.

His firm is dedicated to a singular mission: empowering successful individuals to transition from "rich" to "wealthy" through advanced tax minimization, estate preservation, and multi-generational stewardship.

Chris Heerlein is widely respected for his insights in personal finance and wealth management, and is the author of three books, including *Divorce With Dignity* and *Money Won't Buy Happiness—But Time To Find It*. His latest work, *How To Retire Rich And Look Poor In Retirement*, encapsulates his philosophy of legally disinheriting Uncle Sam to maximize family legacy.

Beyond his work with private clients, Chris is committed to financial education. He is the host of Wealth Radio, a weekly broadcast on Austin's News Radio KLBJ, and the lead contributor to the "Retire Ready" television segment on KXAN News Channel 36.

Chris leads the REAP Financial team from their headquarters in Austin, Texas. He remains dedicated to his firm's founding principle: that true wealth is not just about accumulation, but about the strategic preservation of legacy for generations to come.

Acknowledgments

This book is the result of a journey filled with learning and collaboration, made possible by the incredible support of many individuals. I want to express my sincere gratitude to my family for their unwavering encouragement, understanding, and patience throughout the long hours dedicated to this project. Their belief in me has been a constant source of strength.

To my exceptional team at REAP Financial, I extend my deepest appreciation for their dedication, expertise, and commitment to excellence. The strategies and ideas within these pages have been greatly enriched by their insights and hard work. It is a privilege to work alongside such a talented and passionate group of professionals.

I am also profoundly grateful to my mentor, Jon Powell, whose wisdom and guidance have been transformative. His confidence in my abilities and his insightful perspectives have shaped my professional path and inspired the core principles of this book.

To my readers, as well as the listeners of News Radio KLBJ and the viewers of KXAN News 36, I offer my sincere thanks for trusting me to guide you through the complexities of retirement tax planning for over a decade. This book is my way of expressing my gratitude, providing a resource to help you make informed decisions, strategize to protect your wealth, and achieve the retirement you deserve.

Finally, I wish to acknowledge and thank all those who have supported me along the way—my friends, colleagues, and various experts. Thank you for being an integral part of this journey.

With heartfelt gratitude,
Chris Heerlein

Endnotes

1   John Grobe, "Minimize These Social Security and Medicare 'Taxes,'" *FEDweek*, January 2, 2024, https://www.fedweek.com/tsp/minimize-these-social-security-and-medicare-taxes/.

2   Julia Kagan, "Stealth Taxes: What They Are, How They Work," Investopedia, January 31, 2024, https://www.investopedia.com/terms/s/stealth-taxes.asp.

3   Source of all data on the ultrawealthy (defined as individuals with at least $25 million in net worth, not including value of primary residences): "The $25 Million+ Opportunity: Driving Organic Growth by Attracting, Serving, and Retaining the Ultrawealthy," CEG Insights, September 7, 2023.

4   "The $25 Million+ Opportunity," CEG Insights, 2023

5   Olaya Moldes, "Beyond Experiential Spending: Consumers Report Higher Well-Being from Purchases That Satisfy Intrinsic Goals," *British Journal of Social Psychology* 62, no. 2 (2022), https://doi.org/10.1111/bjso.12602.

6   Underpayment of Estimated Tax by Individuals Penalty | Internal Revenue Service," n.d., https://www.irs.gov/payments/underpayment-of-estimated-tax-by-individuals-penalty.

7   "Suspending Your Retirement Benefit Payments | Social Security Administration," n.d., https://www.ssa.gov/benefits/retirement/planner/suspend.html.

8   Bruce Willey, "How a Backdoor Roth IRA Works (and Its Drawbacks)," Kiplinger, January 13, 2024, https://www.kiplinger.com/retirement/how-a-backdoor-roth-ira-works-and-drawbacks.

9   "Questions and Answers on the Net Investment Income Tax | Internal Revenue Service," n.d., https://www.irs.gov/newsroom/questions-and-answers-on-the-net-investment-income-tax.

10   Income limits change every year so make sure you are working with the most current IRS data.

11   Erica Sandberg, "What Is the Average Retirement Savings Balance by Age?," *US News & World Report*, April 30, 2025, https://money.usnews.com/money/retirement/articles/average-retirement-savings-balance-by-age.

12   Board of Governors of the Federal Reserve System, "Changes in U.S. Family Finances from 2019 to 2022, Evidence from the Survey of Consumer Finances," Federal Reserve Bulletin, October 2023, https://www.federalreserve.gov/publications/files/scf23.pdf.

13   "Roth IRAs," IRS, last updated August 25, 2025, https://www.irs.gov/retirement-plans/Roth-IRAs.

14   Kelley C. Long, "The Ins and Outs of IRA-To-HSA Rollovers," *Journal of Accountancy*, November 29, 2022, https://www.journalofaccountancy.com/news/2022/nov/the-ins-and-outs-IRA-HSA-rollovers.html.

15   John Egan, 2023, "Multi-Year Guaranteed Annuity (MYGA)," *Forbes*, January 11, 2023, https://www.forbes.com/advisor/retirement/multi-year-guaranteed-annuity/.